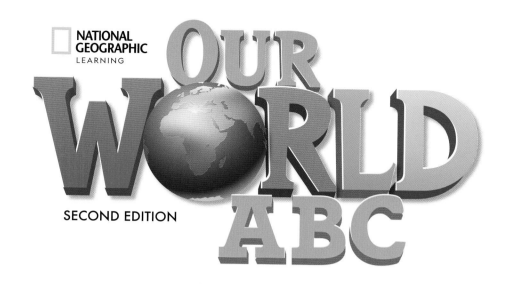

NATIONAL GEOGRAPHIC LEARNING

OUR WORLD ABC

SECOND EDITION

T0349579

SERIES EDITORS
Joan Kang Shin and
JoAnn (Jodi) Crandall

NATIONAL GEOGRAPHIC LEARNING

Australia • Brazil • Mexico • Singapore • United Kingdom • United States

THE ALPHABET

Aa
apple

Bb
baby

Cc
cat

Gg
goat

Hh
hand

Ii
ice cream

Mm
monkey

Nn
nine

Oo
orange

Ss
sock

Tt
turtle

Uu
umbrella

Yy
yellow

Zz
zebra

Dd
dog

Ee
egg

Ff
fish

Jj
jacket

Kk
kite

Ll
lamp

Pp
pencil

Qq
queen

Rr
robot

Vv
vegetables

Ww
water

Xx
fox

Look and listen. Say. TR: 0.1

Trace and match.

Aa

apple

Bb

baby

Cc

cat

Dd

dog

Trace and match.

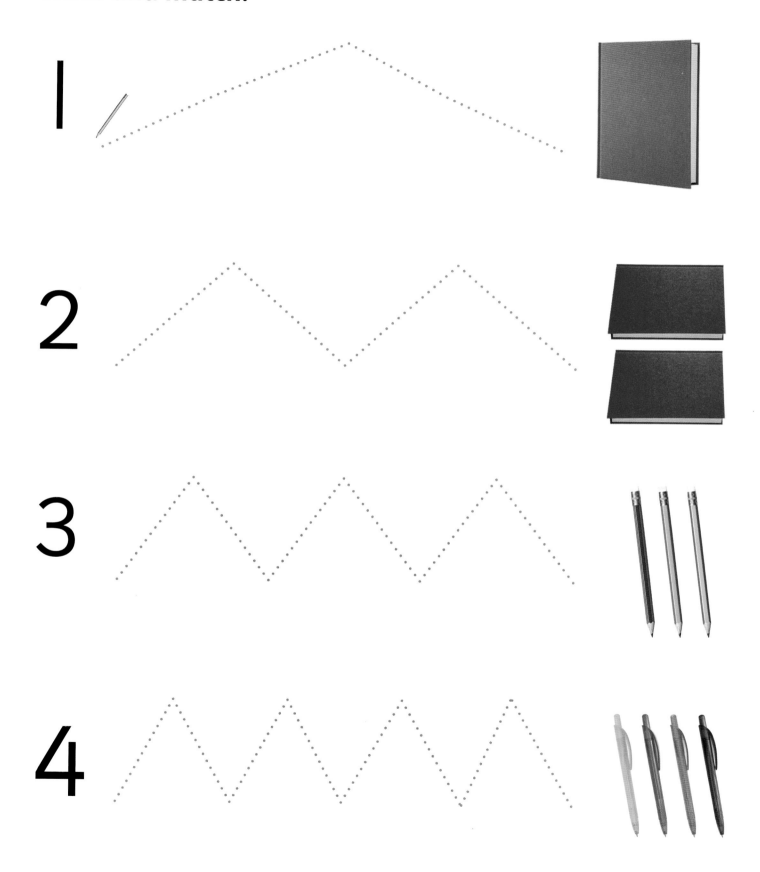

1

2

3

4

Trace.

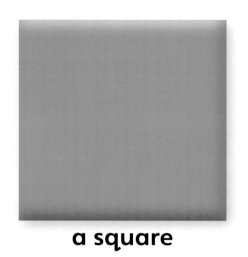

a square

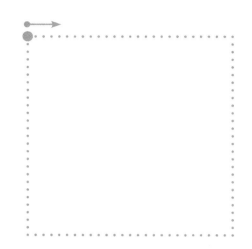

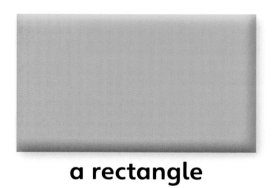

a rectangle

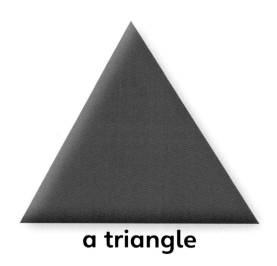

a triangle

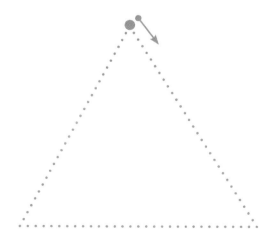

Trace.

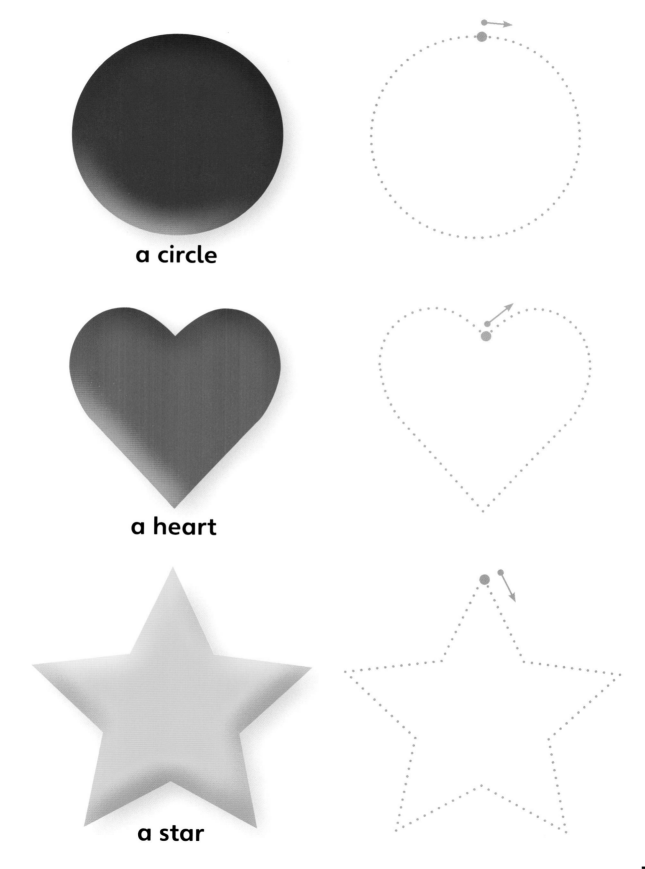

a circle

a heart

a star

Match and trace.

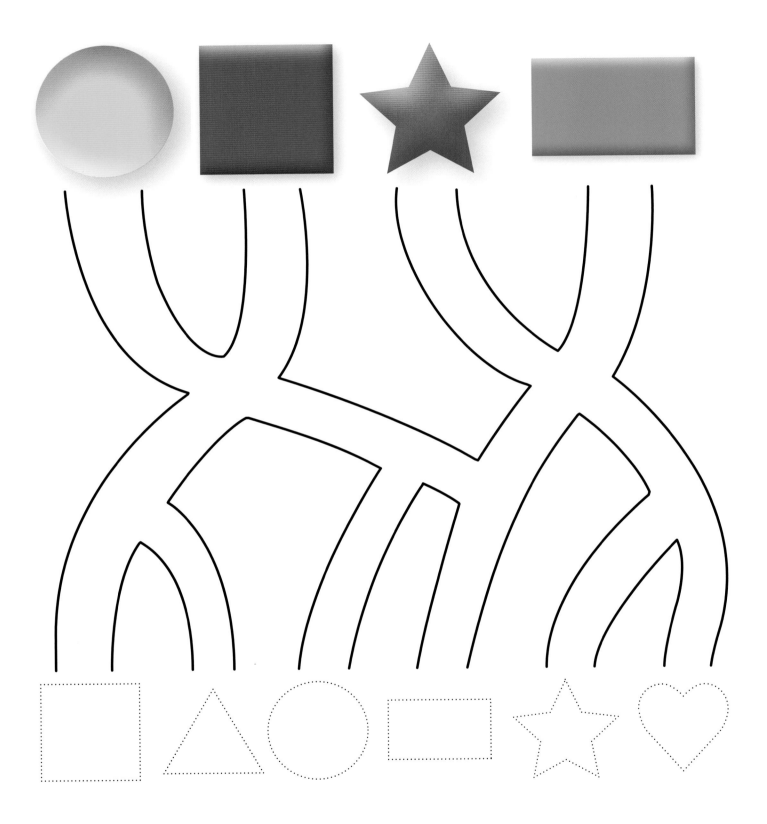

Listen and say. Write. TR: 0.2 and 0.3

a b c d e f g h i j k l m n o p q r s t u v w x y z

a   a   a

A   A   A

apple

b   b   b

B   B   B

baby

Listen and say. Write. TR: 0.4 and 0.5

a b **c d** e f g h i j k l m n o p q r s t u v w x y z

cat

dog

a b c d *e* f g h i j k l m n o p q r s t u v w x y z

e   e   e

egg

E   E   E

f   f   f

fish

F   F   F

Listen and say. Write. TR: 0.8 and 0.9

goat

hand

Listen and say. Write. TR: 0.10 and 0.11

a b c d e f g h **i j** k l m n o p q r s t u v w x y z

i

I

ice cream

j

J

jacket

Listen and say. Write. TR: 0.12 and 0.13

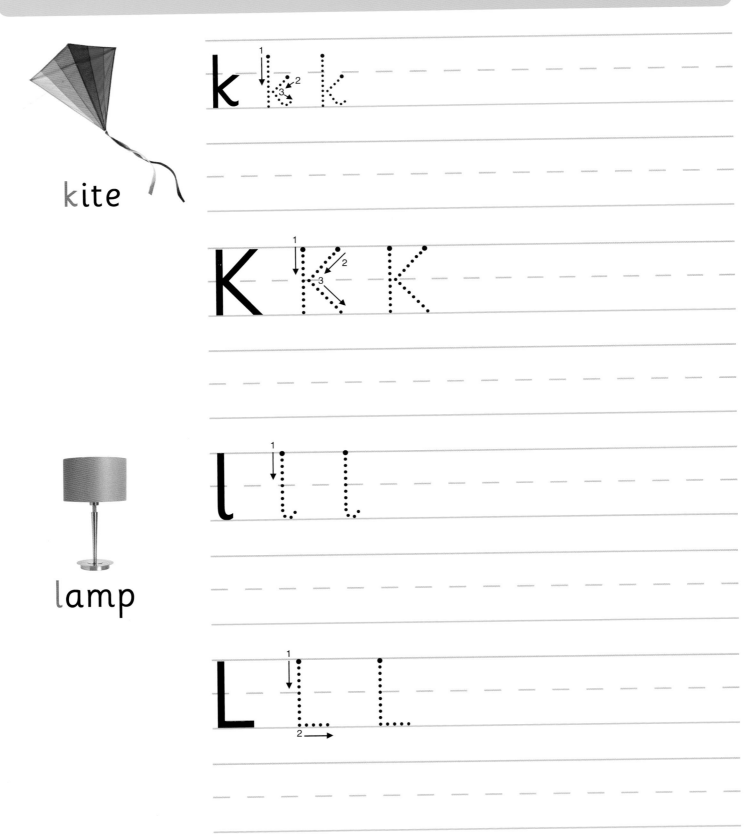

kite

lamp

14

a b c d e f g h i j k l **m n** o p q r s t u v w x y z

m   m   m   m

M   M   M

monkey

n   n   n

N   N   N

9

nine

Listen and say. Write. TR: 0.16 and 0.17

a b c d e f g h i j k l m n **o p** q r s t u v w x y z

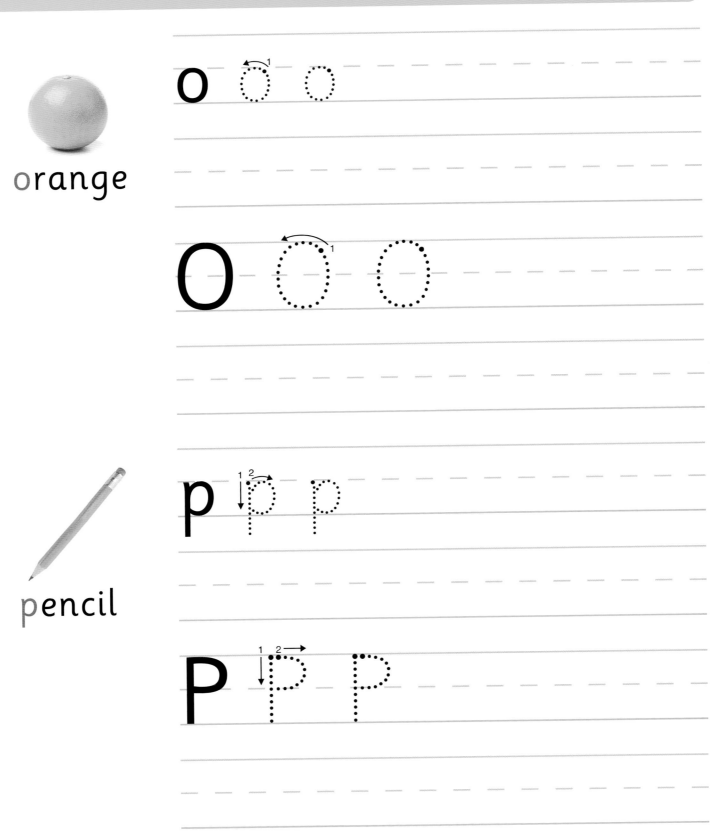

orange

pencil

16

Listen and say. Write. TR: 0.18 and 0.19

a b c d e f g h i j k l m n o p **q** r s t u v w x y z

queen

robot

Listen and say. Write. TR: 0.20 and 0.21

a b c d e f g h i j k l m n o p q r **s t** u v w x y z

sock

turtle

a b c d e f g h i j k l m n o p q r s t **u v** w x y z

u   u u

U   U U

v   v v

umbrella

vegetables

V   V V

Listen and say. Write. TR: 0.24 and 0.25

a b c d e f g h i j k l m n o p q r s t u v **w x** y z

w W w w

W W W W

water

x X x x

X X X X

fox

a b c d e f g h i j k l m n o p q r s t u v w x **y** z

y y y y

yellow

Y Y Y

z z z

Z Z Z

zebra

Listen and say. Write. TR: 0.28

1	2	3	4	5	6	7	8	9	10

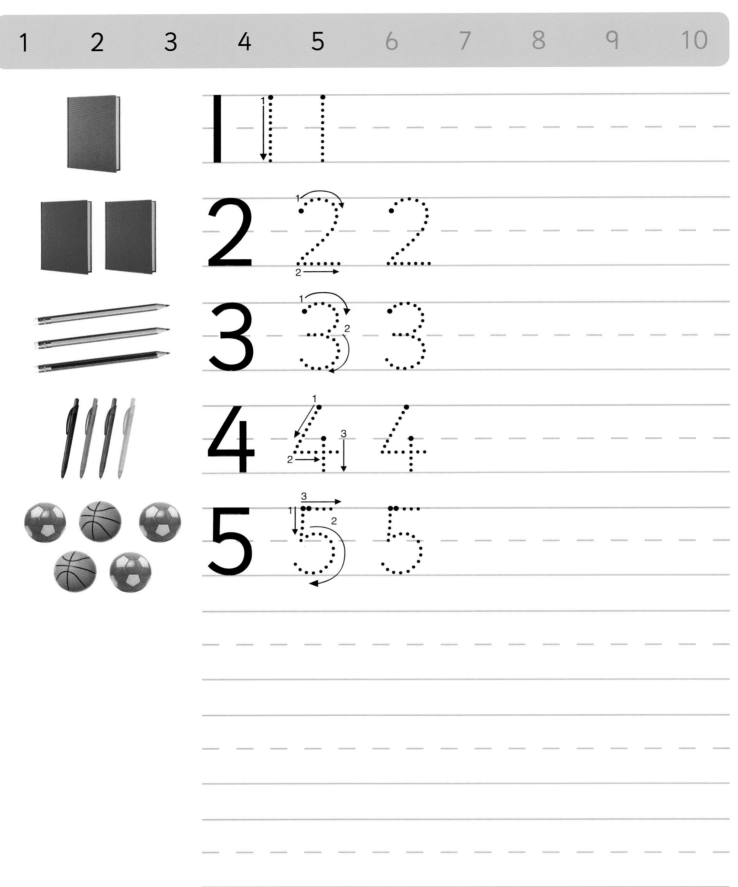

Listen and say. Write. TR: 0.29

| 1 | 2 | 3 | 4 | 5 | 6 | 7 | 8 | 9 | 10 |

6 6 6 — — — — — — —

7 7 7 — — — — — — —

8 8 8 — — — — — — —

9 9 9 — — — — — — —

10 10 10 — — — — — —

Listen and say. Write. TR: 0.30

apple   baby   cat   dog

apple

baby

cat

dog

egg   fish   goat   hand

egg

fish

goat

hand

Listen and say. Write. TR: 0.32

ice cream   jacket   kite   lamp

ice cream

jacket

kite

lamp

Listen and say. Write. TR: 0.33

| monkey | nine | orange | pencil |

monkey

nine

orange

pencil

Listen and say. Write. TR: 0.34

| queen | robot | sock | turtle |

queen

robot

sock

turtle

Listen and say. Write. TR: 0.35

| umbrella | vegetables | water | fox |

umbrella

vegetables

water

fox

Listen and say. Write. TR: 0.36

| yellow | zebra | ! | ? |

yellow

zebra

Hello!

! ↓ ¡

What's your name?

? ? ?

Listen and say. Write. TR: 0.37

| Hello! | What's your name? | My name is _____. |

Hello!

What's your name? name?

My name is

Hello!

What's your name?

My name is Eddie.

Join the dots from a to z and I to I0. Chant. TR: 0.38